# IMAGES
## *of America*
# FLORIDA'S
# GRAND HOTELS
## *from the* GILDED AGE

The grand hotels transformed Florida from a semi-wilderness visited mainly by sportsmen and invalids into a destination for the rich and famous. This portrait from the cover of a brochure promoting the Tampa Bay Hotel shows a fashionable lady on promenade in front of the lavish and exotic structure.

IMAGES
*of America*

# FLORIDA'S
# GRAND HOTELS
*from the* GILDED AGE

R. Wayne Ayers

ARCADIA
PUBLISHING

Copyright © 2005 by R. Wayne Ayers
ISBN-13 978-0-7385-4182-2

Published by Arcadia Publishing
Charleston, South Carolina

Printed in the United States of America

Library of Congress Catalog Card Number: 2005927752

For all general information contact Arcadia Publishing at:
Telephone 843-853-2070
Fax 843-853-0044
E-mail sales@arcadiapublishing.com
For customer service and orders:
Toll-Free 1-888-313-2665

Visit us on the Internet at www.arcadiapublishing.com

*To my wife and grand partner, Nancy, whose creative and organizational genius plus extraordinary ability to interpret my scribbles have made this book a reality.*

# CONTENTS

# ACKNOWLEDGMENTS

The author wishes to thank the following people and organizations for their generous support given to the creation of this book: Susan Carter of the Henry B. Plant Museum, Tampa; Sharon Delahanty of the Belleview-Biltmore, Belleair; Ayumi Iida-Cordon of Heritage Village, Largo; Paul Camp of the University of South Florida, Tampa; James Ponce of The Breakers, Palm Beach; Brian Thompson of Flagler College, St. Augustine; and Adam Watson of the Florida State Archives, Tallahassee.

The author consulted a number of resources, both past and present, in writing the introductory sections and captions for this book. The following publications were especially helpful and are highly recommended to anyone desiring a more in-depth look at the grand hotels featured in this book.

Board, Prudy Taylor and Esther B. Colcord. *The Belleview Mido Resort Hotel: A Century of Hospitality*. Virginia Beach: The Donning Co., 1996.

Braden, Susan R. *The Architecture of Leisure*. Gainesville, FL: University of Florida Press, 2002.

Frisbie, Louise K. *Florida's Fabled Inns*. Bartow, FL: Imperial Publishing Co., 1980.

Graham, Thomas. *Flagler's St. Augustine Hotels*. Sarasota, FL: Pineapple Press, 2004.

Martin, Sidney Walter. *Henry Flagler: Visionary of the Gilded Age*. Lake Buena Vista, FL: Tailored Tours Publications, 1998.

Reynolds, Charles B. *The Standard Guide: St. Augustine*. St. Augustine, FL: Historic Print & Map Co., 1892, reprinted 2004.

Reynolds, Kelly. *Henry Plant: Pioneer Empire Builder*. Cocoa, FL: The Florida Historical Society Press, 2003.

Rhodes, Harrison and Mary Wolfe DuMont. *A Guide to Florida*. New York: Dodd, Mead and Company, 1912.

Turner, Gregg and Seth H. Bramson. *The Plant System of Railroads, Steamships and Hotels*. Laurys Station, PA: Garrigues House, 2004.

# INTRODUCTION

Florida in the late 19th century was a paradise waiting to be discovered. Remote and inaccessible except by steamboat and primitive trails, the territory retained its pioneer status and reputation as a jungle outpost during an era when much of the eastern United States was settling into a comfortable Victorian lifestyle. The state's advantages—two coastlines, tropical splendor, and a mild, balmy winter climate—were largely untapped except at the state's upper reaches, where rail and water transportation had brought some growth to the northeastern corner and parts of the panhandle.

That opening, especially at Jacksonville, where a substantial winter tourist colony was established in the years following the Civil War, was enough to give wealthy socialites and invalids seeking cures for their ailments a taste of the delights of "the land of flowers and sunshine."

Two visionary tycoons, who had amassed the unfettered wealth that accompanied successful pursuits during the Gilded Age, set out in separate ventures that would transform the face of the Sunshine State from a tangled inhospitable jungle into a grand destination for the rich and famous.

Henry M. Flagler saw his opportunity along Florida's East Coast, largely undeveloped beyond Jacksonville, the rail terminus just south of the Georgia border.

Henry B. Plant made his move into Florida down the west side of the peninsula, with rail and steamship lines that would stretch to Tampa and Punta Gorda and seaward to Key West and Cuba. Hotels, including a pair of grand properties, would follow to accommodate the socialites and titans of industry seeking a winter retreat surrounded by splendor.

The seven grand hotels built by Flagler and Plant, five of which survive to this day, are the most visible and lasting legacies of Florida's elegant frontier and its creators.

Separately but with a common goal, these two magnates of the Gilded Age would establish Florida's resort locations in the late 19th century and build an infrastructure for tourism that would carry forward to the 21st century.

Both Flagler and Plant thought in grand terms, and the empires they built to bring their visions to reality, from transportation systems to accommodations, were on a grand scale.

A honeymoon visit to Jacksonville and the ancient city of St. Augustine by Standard Oil tycoon Henry Flagler and his new bride, Ida Alice, proved to be the catalyst that would open the frontier regions of coastal Florida to booming development.

The Florida sojourn during the brutal northern winter of 1883–1884 left a deep impression on Flagler, and the couple made plans for a return to St. Augustine the following winter. Changes that Flagler noted in St. Augustine during the couple's 1885 visit—the opening of the plain but luxurious San Marco Hotel and new rail transportation that gave the city greater accessibility—kindled Flagler's visionary spirit.

Soon Flagler was stirring with grandiose plans for a hotel of his own that would be followed by another and the acquisition of a third. The Ponce de Leon, Flagler's crown jewel, was completed on May 30, 1887, barely three years after the honeymooning couple's first sight of the area.

Flagler started his second hotel property in early 1887, while the Ponce de Leon was still under construction. The Spanish Renaissance-style Alcazar, less elaborate than the Ponce de Leon, was designed by Flagler to serve a clientele of more modest means. Flagler completed his triumvirate of St. Augustine hotel properties with his purchase of the Casa Monica in 1889, renaming it the Cordova. Entertainment and recreation facilities located at the Alcazar served guests of all three hotels.

In two years, Flagler had transformed the oldest city in North America from a sleepy military outpost and curiosity into a burgeoning tourist destination offering first-class accommodations and resort amenities. The Flagler hotels, all within a block of one another near the heart of St. Augustine, became the attraction in a city known for its abundance of venerable sights.

Meanwhile Flagler's vision extended southward to the vast unreached regions of warmer climes, unclaimed coastline, and tropical splendor. His focus shifted to transportation, for Florida's roads were largely primitive wagon trails, and railroads, where they existed, were poor. Development of the enticing tracts of virgin South Florida land would not come without access.

During the 1880s, Flagler began to acquire and upgrade a series of short narrow-gauge railroads in northeast Florida, and he built a modern depot in St. Augustine near his Ponce de Leon hotel.

By the late 19th century, Flagler's vision was expanding down the east coast toward ever warmer and more lush environs. His rail line pushed forward, south to Daytona and Ormond, where he purchased and expanded the Ormond Beach Hotel.

The mid-1890s saw Flagler's Florida East Coast Railway extend to Palm Beach, where he was to make his grandest statement with the opening in 1894 of the Hotel Royal Poinciana, the largest hotel in the world. With accommodations for 1,200 guests, the Royal Poinciana quickly became the winter gathering place for a mixed clientele that included the movers and shakers of the day along with guests of less affluent means.

The wealthy socialite guests of the leisure class often spent the entire winter season—January through March—at the hotel, filling their days and nights with rounds of parties, golf, afternoon teas, concerts, strolling, or being transported around the extensive grounds in wheeled chairs, sometimes called Afromobiles, powered by hotel employees.

The Royal Poinciana continued to be a prime destination during the Gilded Age, but it began to decline in the 1920s and finally closed in 1931. The structure was razed in 1934.

At Palm Beach, Flagler built his first and only hotel located directly on the beach—The Breakers, which opened as the Palm Beach Inn. The hotel was renamed The Breakers in 1900 after an extensive remodeling. That structure would last only three years, burning down in 1903. The Breakers that emerged in 1904 was, like its predecessor, U-shaped to take full advantage of its beachfront location by offering ocean views from most guest rooms. This structure lasted until 1925 when it too succumbed to fire.

Lushly landscaped grounds ran the half-mile distance between the Royal Poinciana and The Breakers, offering guests the opportunity for a stroll or ride in the wheeled bicycle chairs.

A series of disastrous freezes in the winter of 1894–1895 that extended to Palm Beach caused Flagler to consider extending his Florida East Coast Railway farther south. Prominent Miami pioneer, entrepreneur, and landowner Julia Tuttle saw an opportunity to entice Flagler to the then-struggling outpost on Biscayne Bay. She sent Flagler bouquets of orange blossoms following the freezes, and more importantly, she offered a substantial portion of her prime land holdings along the Miami River.

Tuttle's entreaties had their desired effect, and on April 21, 1896, the first train of the Florida East Coast Railway pulled into Miami. Groundbreaking for what was to be Flagler's southernmost hotel to date had been a month earlier, and in January 1897, the sweeping five-story Royal Palm, with accommodations for 700 guests and a dining room seating 500 people, opened in the town of Miami, population 2,000.

Flagler devoted 15 acres of prime land at the mouth of the Miami River to the hotel. The imposing structure, with its elegant appointments, modern amenities, and richly landscaped grounds, was a world apart from the surrounding pioneer village and Everglade wilds. The property proved to be a resounding hit with a leisure class eager to experience luxury in a locale far off the beaten track. According to one account, the Royal Palm hosted "some of the richest and most famous people in the world."

Flagler went on to build or acquire several smaller hotel properties in other Florida localities, but his greatest contribution to Florida tourism was bringing grand luxury accommodations along with rail transportation to the East Coast. That accomplishment put Florida at the top of the grand tour for gilded travelers.

By the time of his death in 1913, Flagler owned nine hotels in Florida, including the six grand properties focused on in this book.

While Henry Flagler was at work transforming the east coast of Florida, another business tycoon of the Gilded Age was stirring with grandiose plans for the primitive frontier of the state's west coast.

Henry B. Plant began to assemble the transportation empire that would stretch into Florida during the South's Reconstruction period following the Civil War. Like Flagler, Plant got his first taste of the state's amenities at Jacksonville, where he arrived in 1853 with his young wife, Ellen, seeking a cure for her worsening tuberculosis. Unlike his East Coast rival, Henry Plant spent his career in transportation, beginning as a cabin boy in steamers operating from ports in his native New England. During the War Between the States, Plant bought out the Southern assets of the Harnden Express Company, where he was superintendent, and formed the Southern Express Company.

Following the conflict, Plant began to invest in rail lines along the devastated Southern Seaboard states. Plant made his first big rail deal in 1879, acquiring the Atlantic and Gulf Railroad, which ran through Georgia and gave him access into Florida at Jacksonville and Live Oak. By 1883, Plant had the competing Florida Southern Railway under wraps and had big plans for extending the line down the peninsula.

Acquisition of additional rail and steamboat lines followed, and in 1884, Plant's transportation network reached Tampa, which would be the site of his flagship hotel property, the grand Tampa Bay Hotel.

Plant began construction of what would be his favorite hotel and grandest statement in 1888. Completed in 1891 at a cost of nearly $3 million, the structure was a sight to behold. Following Plant's utilitarian Inn at Port Tampa, the sprawling edifice of the Tampa Bay Hotel was a masterpiece of ornate and fanciful design even by Gilded Age standards. The five-story red-brick Moorish "palace" was topped by 13 silvered onion domes and minarets each bearing a crescent moon representing a month of the Muslim year. The awesome structure was to become the defining element of the Tampa skyline for years to come.

Plant spared no expense in the design, construction, and furnishing of his landmark property, said to have been his pride and joy. The entire hotel was lighted inside and out with electricity, considered a rare luxury at the time even in more sophisticated locales. Close to $1 million was spent by Plant in furnishing the hotel's guest rooms and parlors with antiques and period pieces, many selected personally by Plant and his second wife, Margaret, during their travels to Europe.

Over 2,000 people attended the hotel's gala grand-opening celebration on February 5, 1891. "The Brilliance and Beauty of the Scene Surpass the Poet's Dream and Defy Description," a headline in the *Tampa Daily Journal* enthused over the event. The correspondent went on to describe "a beautiful building with its turrets, domes and minarets towering heavenward and glistening in the sun" during the day; and an even more impressive nighttime scene, with the hotel illuminated by electricity and "the grounds and flower plats lit with Chinese lanterns and fairy candles of every hue . . . the whole forming a scene of dazzling light and beauty that the pen of a genius could not truthfully portray."

While the Tampa Bay Hotel met every expectation of the leisure class for grandeur, comfort, amenities, and Gilded Age splendor, its financial success was more problematical.

The hotel's construction costs were $500,000 over budget, and day-to-day operation proved far more expensive than anticipated. The facility proved to be a colossal drain on the Plant System's bottom line, even while still remaining the twinkle in Plant's gilded eye.

In 1905, six years after Henry Plant's death and following 14 years of mixed financial returns, Plant's heirs sold his legendary property to the City of Tampa. Today, the Henry B. Plant Museum preserves the south wing of the structure, now home to the University of Tampa, with original furnishings and artifacts that tell the story of Plant's masterpiece to future generations.

Plant began work on his second grand hotel, the Hotel Belleview, in 1896, some four years after the Tampa Bay Hotel was completed. A secluded site on a bluff overlooking Clearwater Bay, near the Gulf of Mexico, was personally chosen by Plant as the location for his new luxury property. Plant envisioned a planned community, called Belleair, which would be developed around the hotel site.

The Belleview would be a dramatic departure in both concept and style from Plant's formal, fantastical red-brick Tampa Bay Hotel. In keeping with its scenic, remote setting, the Belleview's style would be more relaxed and informal, with outdoor amenities such as golf, bicycling, horseback riding, and fishing supplanting the performing arts as the focal point of activity. A livery stable on the property operated until 1950.

The hotel was constructed entirely of wood, which was Florida heart pine, with peaked roofs evocative of the Swiss chalet-style architecture coming into vogue in mountain and seaside resorts. The finished structure would be more appropriately described as picturesque rather than fantastical.

Plant brought a spur of his railroad down from Clearwater to the door of the hotel, assuring easy access for Gilded Age tourists, a number of whom would arrive in private railcars. A section of track was even extended to the hotel basement for delivery of supplies and baggage.

The Belleview's rustic get-away-from-it-all aura had a special appeal for gilded guests seeking refuge from the rigors of the Industrial Age who nonetheless expected and were provided with the most up-to-date amenities and luxuries of the day. The hotel's accoutrements included electric lighting, telephone and telegraph services, and an in-house barbershop. In a bow to culture, an in-house orchestra performed daily.

The Belleview was an immediate success, and later additions, including the construction of two new wings, would increase the hotel's capacity from 145 rooms to 425.

Under the stewardship of Henry Plant's son, Morton, who took over operation of the property following the patriarch's unexpected death in 1899, the hotel experienced its greatest period of growth and prosperity. While Henry Plant considered the Tampa Bay Hotel his pride, Morton's favorite was said to be the Belleview.

The emerging sport of golf was to play a big role among the Belleview's attractions. A six-hole course in place when the Belleview opened was Florida's first golf course.

Morton Plant ensured the Belleview's ongoing reputation as a renowned golf resort in 1915, when he hired famed golf-course designer Donald J. Ross to create two 18-hole championship courses for the hotel. Judging the Florida soil unsuitable for greens, Plant imported topsoil from Indiana to create the perfect putting surface.

The Belleview's Gilded Age guests included presidents, corporate tycoons, international dignitaries, celebrities, socialites, and other patrons who appreciated the hotel's splendid isolation. The hotel was nicknamed "The White Queen of the Gulf" after being painted white in the early 20th century and took the name Belleview Biltmore in 1919.

Though the hotel would experience ups and downs through the years, including a bankruptcy filing during the Depression years, the Belleview Biltmore remains to this day a first class hostelry in the grand tradition.

The Plant empire would grow and include hotel properties along Plant's railroads in Winter Park (The Seminole), Ocala (The Ocala House), Punta Gorda (Hotel Punta Gorda), and later Fort Myers (Fort Myers Hotel), but none would achieve the grand status and notoriety accorded Henry and Morton Plant's favorite creations—the Tampa Bay Hotel and the Belleview.

"Every comfort and pleasure" was promised to tourists as an enticement to spend the winter in Florida at one of Flagler's grand hotels. Advertisements like this one featuring the Ponce de Leon in St. Augustine were run regularly in publications read by the elite leisure class.

# One

# ST. AUGUSTINE
## *Ponce de Leon, Alcazar, and Cordova*

Flagler's first and most grandiose hotel was the Ponce de Leon, which opened in 1888 shortly after Flagler extended his rail line from Jacksonville to St. Augustine. Flagler spent $2.5 million to construct his premier hotel, making it the most expensive hotel building in the world, and he spared no expense in its appointments. Since 1969, the Ponce de Leon has been the home of Flagler College.

The hotel featured lushly landscaped grounds and a plaza that it was to share with Flagler's neighboring properties, the Alcazar and Cordova. The expansive hotel covered six acres and contained over two miles of corridors. Here horse-drawn carriages line up at the Ponce de Leon's entrance to drop off and transport guests.

Construction of the Ponce de Leon began December 1, 1885, and the hotel was completed a year and a half later, too late for the 1887 season. The site for the hotel was created by filling in marshland with sand and removing several buildings from the property. (Courtesy of Flagler College.)

This view shows the building of the rotunda, the lavish showplace entry to the hotel. The temporary railways laid down along the city streets to transport the mammoth amount of materials used in the hotel's construction can be seen on the right. (Courtesy of Flagler College.)

When complete, the Ponce de Leon would provide stiff competition for the Hotel San Marco, St. Augustine's first hotel built on a grand scale. Opened in 1884, the San Marco impressed Flagler when he stayed there with new bride, Ida Alice, during the winter of 1885. Flagler would hire the San Marco's New York architects, James McGuire and Joseph McDonald, to build the hotel and would later spirit away the San Marco's esteemed manager, Osborn D. Seavey, to run his new property. (Courtesy of Florida State Archives.)

During his early stays in St. Augustine, Flagler visited the city's annual Ponce de Leon celebration. The event was held along the downtown waterfront and drew huge crowds each year, and it helped convince Flagler of the area's viability as a tourist attraction.

The Spanish castle-style architecture of Villa Zorayda, with its concrete-wall construction, would serve as a model for Flagler in the building of the Ponce de Leon. The structure was designed by Boston philanthropist Franklin W. Smith as his winter residence. Smith also designed the Cordova Hotel, which Flagler would later own. Smith and Flagler partnered to build a hotel in the city but later had a falling out and ended their association.

The Ponce de Leon's architecture was a mixture of Moorish, Spanish, and Italian influences, a concoction that would captivate the tastes of a public already swept with a craze for Eastern exotic. The Ponce de Leon would become the first large structure in America to be constructed from poured concrete, which was mixed with coquina shell quarried from nearby Anastasia Island. Note the planked sidewalks on the right in this early view. (Courtesy of Flagler College.)

Wide-arched verandas flanked the courtyard and provided a shaded place for guests to sit and enjoy the view. (Courtesy of Flagler College.)

A lushly landscaped plaza, shown here under construction in 1888, fronted the Ponce de Leon and would connect the hotel with the entertainment and recreation complex in the Hotel Alcazar, which Flagler started shortly after the Ponce de Leon's completion. The unkempt, rutted condition of Cordova Street (on the right) and other St. Augustine roadways was a constant source of irritation and frustration for Flagler and was said to play a major role in his decision to eventually direct his attention southward to Palm Beach. (Courtesy of Flagler College.)

The Hotel Ponce de Leon was the wonder of St. Augustine and captured the nation's attention when it opened to great fanfare on January 10, 1888. Celebration events included balls, dinners, and parties where locals mixed with the New York elite, who arrived in private railroad cars supplied by Flagler. Thousands of electric lights supplied the glow for a glittering three-day occasion. (Courtesy of Flagler College.)

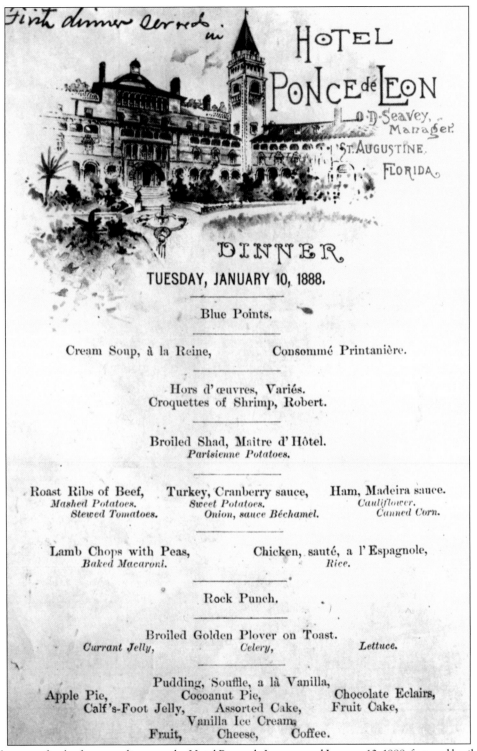

*First dinner served in*

# HOTEL PONCE de LEON

O. D. Seavey,
Manager.
ST. AUGUSTINE,
FLORIDA.

## DINNER

### TUESDAY, JANUARY 10, 1888.

Blue Points.

Cream Soup, à la Reine,          Consommé Printanière.

Hors d' œuvres, Variés.
Croquettes of Shrimp, Robert.

Broiled Shad, Maitre d' Hôtel.
*Parisienne Potatoes.*

Roast Ribs of Beef,      Turkey, Cranberry sauce,      Ham, Madeira sauce.
*Mashed Potatoes.*            *Sweet Potatoes.*                *Cauliflower.*
*Stewed Tomatoes.*        *Onion, sauce Béchamel.*              *Canned Corn.*

Lamb Chops with Peas,          Chicken, sauté, a l' Espagnole,
*Baked Macaroni.*                          *Rice.*

Rock Punch.

Broiled Golden Plover on Toast.
*Currant Jelly,*              *Celery,*              *Lettuce.*

Pudding, Souffle, a là Vanilla,
Apple Pie,          Cocoanut Pie,          Chocolate Eclairs,
Calf's-Foot Jelly,      Assorted Cake,      Fruit Cake,
Vanilla Ice Cream,
Fruit,          Cheese,          Coffee.

The menu for the first-ever dinner at the Hotel Ponce de Leon served January 10, 1888, featured broiled golden plover and rock punch among other specialties. (Courtesy of Florida State Archives.)

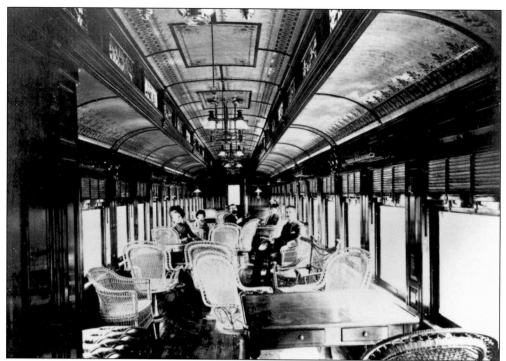

The opening of the Ponce de Leon coincided with Flagler's bringing of first-class railway service to St. Augustine. Arrival of the first vestibule train on opening day signaled the city's accessibility to gilded patrons who could now travel in style to reach the paradise resort Flagler had prepared for them. (Courtesy of Delaware Public Archives.)

During the season, the Florida East Coast Railway depot in St. Augustine was often crowded with carriages ready to take arriving passengers to their winter stay in the tropics.

Henry Flagler's private rail car, Number 90, shown here in 1898, could be spotted on the tracks traveling between Flagler's Northern and Florida interests. Other gilded guests who frequented the hotels, such as members of the Vanderbilt and Rockefeller families, would also arrive in their private cars. (Courtesy of Delaware Public Archives.)

This glimpse into the interior of Flagler's private car shows its rich appointments. (Courtesy of Delaware Public Archives.)

The Ponce de Leon would host a number of gatherings of elite and socially prominent citizens during the hotel's years of prominence in the late 19th century. Here a group gathers in the rotunda with Flagler and his wife, Ida Alice (both center front). (Courtesy of Flagler College.)

Here a lady removes her hat as she is assisted from the steps of one of the Flagler railway cars. (Courtesy of Florida State Archives.)

The Ponce de Leon's grand main entrance was flanked by heraldic lion heads, symbol of the Spanish town of Leon, which withstood an attack by Moors during the Middle Ages. The lion was also a symbol of Juan Ponce de Leon, who was proclaimed "a lion in name and heart." The entry gate was raised to great ceremony at the beginning of the winter season and also shut with fanfare at the season's end in mid-April.

The hotel was entered through a lushly landscaped courtyard. The grand entrance can be seen in the center behind the fountain. The east and west entrances are hidden in the foliage.

23

The centerpiece of the courtyard, or Fountain Court, is this ornate fountain surrounded by a group of water-spitting frogs. Note the girl in the foreground with a tiny pet on a leash.

"Aunt Belle" shows off her Victorian finery at a scenic spot in the courtyard. (Courtesy of Flagler College.)

The courtyard was divided into geometric squares after the Spanish manner. The twin towers of Flagler's Alcazar Hotel can be seen to the upper left. Flagler once said that the greatest challenge of his Florida endeavors was the building of the Ponce de Leon—how to keep the hotel in character with its historic surroundings while meeting the demands for the latest amenities expected by his wealthy socialite guests. (Courtesy of Flagler College.)

Concerts by the hotel's house orchestra were given daily in the courtyard.

The Ponce de Leon's magnificent four-story rotunda provided a grand introduction to the hotel's splendor and refinement. The mosaic floor tiles were done by Italian artisans. On the ceiling, renowned muralist George Maynard created female figures in personification of fire, water, air, and earth, and also adventure, discover, conquest, and civilization.

The grand parlor was the hotel's center for parties and balls. This formal affair is being hosted by Mrs. Flagler, pictured in the center with crown and roses. Five U.S. presidents—Grover Cleveland, William McKinley, Theodore Roosevelt, Warren Harding, and Lyndon Johnson—were visitors at the Ponce de Leon. (Courtesy of Flagler College.)

Just beyond the rotunda, stairs of marble and Mexican onyx led to the hotel's elegant main dining room. The wall and ceiling murals depicting classical figures, along with the room's rich appointments and sheer expansiveness (800 guests could be seated), gave visitors a sense of awe. While feasting on the house specialties, diners would be serenaded by members of the hotel orchestra playing from two musicians' galleries overhanging the hall. (Courtesy of Florida State Archives.)

Louis Tiffany was hired as decorator for the hotel and supplied the famed stained glass. It was said that each room cost $1,000 to furnish. This view of the ladies' parlor, with its onyx mantle fireplace, portrays the lavishness of the hotel's décor. The parlor was a place for female guests to engage in the more refined pursuits of reading, sewing, music, and the like, apart from the billiards playing and cigar smoking that took place in the men's parlor down the hall.

Children's activities included events in the hotel's outdoor Palm Garden. (Courtesy of Flagler College.)

The Ponce de Leon's fame made the hotel a popular venue for making motion pictures, a novelty when this silent production was filmed around 1910. (Courtesy of Florida State Archives.)

Omnibuses, which ran on rail lines fronting the hotels, transported visitors to sites and attractions around town.

Flagler planned his second St. Augustine hotel, the Alcazar, to appeal to a less affluent clientele than the Ponce de Leon. The hotel cost only half as much to build as the Ponce de Leon and offered less lavish appointments, although it did have recreational amenities such as a swimming pool. The 300-room structure, which sat across a landscaped plaza from its sister hotel, was likened to a Spanish castle or citadel.

A major attraction of the Alcazar was its entertainment complex, which featured a casino, Turkish baths, tennis courts, and the bathing pool shown here. The pool served as the centerpiece of the complex, which was used by guests of the three Flagler hotels in the vicinity. An upper-floor ballroom surrounding the pool was the venue for plays and concerts. The hotel band played afternoons at the pool, while the evening's amusement featured high dives and swimming feats. (Courtesy of Florida State Archives.)

This c. 1893 view shows the Alcazar, with its bold fortress appearance, as seen from the portico of the Ponce de Leon. The building is now the Lightner Museum, a noted St. Augustine attraction that displays works of art and other treasures. (Courtesy of Florida State Archives.)

This view of the Alcazar's ladies' parlor shows a richly appointed interior, though the hotel lacked the classical splendor that Flagler lavished on the Ponce de Leon.

The Alcazar courtyard featured a fountain and reflecting pool. Shops, offices, and restaurants were located in the alcoves surrounding the court, a feature that has been maintained to this day. The name Alcazar is taken from the Arab word Al-Kasr, or House of Caesar, which referred to the Alcazar Palace of Seville, Spain.

This group of bicyclists has gathered at the hotel tennis courts preparing for a ride. During the 1890s, when this photograph was taken, bicycling ranked with golf and tennis as the most popular recreation engaged in by the leisure class. A couple sporting a bicycle built for two can be seen in the foreground. (Courtesy of Florida State Archives.)

The new Opera House, St. Augustine, Fla.

The Opera House, located across from the Ponce de Leon, offered an added entertainment venue for hotel guests. An amazing new form of theater—moving pictures—came to the stage of the Alcazar Casino in 1898.

The Alcazar, with its in-house entertainment and recreation facilities, proved to be a popular choice for St. Augustine visitors. In some years, the hotel actually attracted more guests than its highly touted ritzy neighbor across the plaza. In 1903, the hotel would be expanded when the Cordova next door ceased to operate as an independent hotel and became the Alcazar Annex.

Flagler bought his third St. Augustine hotel property, the Cordova (Casa Monica), from original owner Franklin W. Smith four months after it opened in January 1888. Ironically the hotel never earned a profit for Flagler, but it stands today as the highly rated Casa Monica resort and is the only Flagler property still operated as a hotel.

The Cordova opened its doors as the Casa Monica in 1888 only a few days after the Ponce de Leon, and it was destined to operate in the shadow of its more famous and well-publicized neighbor. While crowds witnessed the Ponce de Leon's arrival, the Cordova opened with only a handful of guests. Flagler bought the hotel from owner Franklin W. Smith at the end of the 1888 winter season and renamed it the Cordova.

The Cordova, with its Moorish style of architecture, fit well with Flagler's neighboring hotels. Promotional brochures touted the entertainment and recreation facilities available at the Alcazar next door. The hotel was reasonably well patronized during its early years, and this view shows carriages lined up both at the Ponce de Leon in the foreground and at the Cordova. (Courtesy of Florida State Archives.)

The Cordova's public rooms were well appointed, reflecting improvements that Flagler made after acquiring the property. This 1891 view shows the hotel's parlor. An advertisement for the hotel also mentions a sun parlor that is 108 feet long "paved with tiles and roofed with glass." (Courtesy of Florida State Archives.)

As the weakest of Flagler's St. Augustine hotel triumvirate, the Cordova suffered most when Flagler shifted his focus southward to Palm Beach in the late 19th century. In 1903, a bridge was built over Cordova Street connecting the hotel to the Alcazar, and the Cordova became an annex of its more successful neighbor.

Shops of many descriptions, including the world's largest collection of postcards, a drug store, and Persian Bazaar, were located along King Street neighboring the Cordova. The Ponce de Leon's twin towers can be seen on the right.

Flagler built Memorial Presbyterian Church, pictured here in the foreground, as a tribute to his much loved daughter, Jennie Louise, who died on March 25, 1889, after a period of ill health. Her death occurred as she was traveling on a recuperative trip to St. Augustine aboard a yacht owned by her father-in-law. The church was designed by Carrere and Hastings, architects of the Ponce de Leon and Alcazar hotels. Flagler's body is interred in a vault near his daughter in the mausoleum adjoining the church.

Golf was an important amenity offered by the hotels and was a fashionable sport ideally suited to the warm and bracing Florida winter climate. Course challenges in the flat Florida terrain included innovations like this tower fashioned from coquina rock that formed the Number 4 tee at Flagler's St. Augustine links. The golf course was situated on marshy land at the southern tip of the peninsula, a location that often forced players to base their tee times on the daily tide schedule.

TREASURY STREET, ST. AUGUSTINE, FLA.

NARROWEST IN U. S., 6 FEET, 1 INCH          31512

Visitors to St. Augustine at the turn of the century had plenty of historical attractions and curiosities to visit, including Treasury Street, the narrowest street in the United States. The site is still a popular tourist venue.

The city's fabled gates form the backdrop for this gag photograph of Florida governor William S. Jennings (right) taking a test ride in a gator-powered "Florida Automobile." (Courtesy of Florida State Archives.)

St. George Street, with its quaint Spanish architecture, was a place for a stroll or a carriage ride. A millinery store is on the right.

Victorian St. Augustine offered competing "oldest houses." Whitney's oldest house, pictured here, was located on the south end of Hospital Street.

The interior of Whitney's oldest house, claimed to have been built in 1510, shows its age in this 1904 photograph. The museum contained an eclectic mix of curiosities, including a stuffed gator, a rattler, horseshoe crabs, and other seashore artifacts. Most likely the man in the chair is Mr. Whitney. It was later determined that the house dated only to the early 19th century.

The Vedder House was acquired by the St. Augustine Historical Society in 1899 and made into a museum. The sign under the window to the right identifies the structure as the "old house." The building burned down in 1914. The Historical Society also purchased the Gonzalez-Alvarez House on St. Francis Street, which is the only one of the three "oldest" houses that can actually be dated to the 16th century. It has been exhibited as "The Oldest House" since 1892 and can still be toured today.

The Plaza, later called Cathedral Place as it fronted the cathedral on the north, is the city's public park and dates to Revolutionary War times. The Ponce de Leon's towers can be seen in the distance in this view dating c. 1900.

ST. AUGUSTINE, Fla. from Matanzas River.

*I hope you are all well. Yours sincerely Fannie B. B.*

St. Augustine's picturesque waterfront on the Matanzas River was a short walk from the Flagler hotels. Guests could view the many watercraft plying the river or perhaps take a ride in one of the vessels.

Bridge across Matanzas River at St. Augustine, Fla.

Across the river lay the attractions of Anastasia Island, reached by this wooden bridge. The sign at the ticket office on the left promises fine bicycling on the island and lists the following attractions: lighthouse, jetties, quarries, and "no better beach anywhere." Note the train engine and car that offered transit across the bridge. The cart in the foreground is from the Hotel Supply Company.

Anastasia Lighthouse, located on Anastasia Island one mile from the city, was a popular tourist attraction as well as a first-order working lighthouse. Today the structure continues to draw visitors who can climb to the top and also tour the fine museum located on the property.

This postcard shows a couple relaxing on the grounds of Fort Marion. The fort, built by the Spanish in 1756 and located just north of the city, is an antiquity popular with tourists then as well as now.

Empire builder Henry M. Flagler evokes a tender moment in this encounter with his dog, Delos, on the Ponce de Leon's veranda. (Courtesy of Flagler College.)

## Two

# PALM BEACH
## Hotel Royal Poinciana and The Breakers

The Hotel Royal Poinciana at Palm Beach, said to be the largest resort hotel in the world when it opened in 1894, was Flagler's showplace. The scene is captured on an alligator-border postcard, a series that was popular with tourists visiting Florida in the early 20th century. A number of scenes were created, all featuring the distinctive gator motif. Today the cards are highly valued collector items and often command high prices when offered for sale.

Flagler chose Palm Beach, a desolate barrier island about 250 miles south of St. Augustine, as the site for his most spectacular property, the Royal Poinciana. The hotel, built at the then-termination point of Flagler's Florida East Coast Railway, became a magnet for the social elite and established Palm Beach as the premier resort destination for the rich and famous. A spur of the railroad delivered guests right to the hotel's door. This gathering of high society included famed business tycoon Cornelius Vanderbilt, on the right. (Courtesy of Florida State Archives.)

Materials used in building the immense structure included 1,400 kegs of nails, 5 million feet of lumber, 360,000 shingles, 4,000 barrels of lime, 500,000 bricks, 2,400 gallons of paint, 20 acres of plaster, 1,200 windows, and 1,800 doors.

The Royal Poinciana proved so popular that it was enlarged twice, doubling its size with each expansion. By the early 20th century, the hotel could accommodate 2,000 guests who were well looked after by nearly 1,700 employees. (Courtesy of Florida State Archives.)

Guests dressed in their Victorian finery relax on the Colonnade of the Royal Poinciana. The hotel was described in an early guidebook as "a city under one roof, with a corridor like a street of small shops, innumerable public rooms, various restaurants, vast piazzas, all filled with a gay, idle, and well-dressed cosmopolitan throng."

The Poinciana's lush tropical grounds that stretched half a mile to Flagler's oceanfront Breakers hotel were a special attraction. Walkways traversed the towering palms and other botanical delights, and guests were transported in bicycle chairs powered by hotel employees. (Courtesy of Florida State Archives.)

The wheeled chairs pictured here were the only form of transportation allowed on the island for years aside from a lone mule car. The vehicles were sometimes referred to as "Afromobiles" as most of the "drivers," all hotel employees, were black.

A favorite wheeled-chair excursion was the jungle trail, a three-mile stretch through dense vegetation. Charges for the pedicycles, which were wicker chairs attached to a bicycle frame, were $1 an hour plus tips. A guidebook warned that the expense of the chairs could mount up to a considerable sum but added, "Palm Beach does not put one in the mood for economy."

Solid Comfort in Palm Beach, Fla.

The Dock, Hotel Royal Poinciana, Palm Beach, Fla.

The wooden pier jutting into Lake Worth provided opportunities for fishing, boat rides, or taking a leisurely stroll.

Henry M. Flagler takes a ride with his dog, Delos, in his private leather-upholstered chair. Powering the vehicle is Flagler's personal valet, George Conway. (Courtesy of Florida State Archives.)

Coconut Grove featured afternoon teas and outdoor events relished by the refined clientele of the Royal Poinciana seeking escape from the wintry North. Activities offered by the hotel were varied and plentiful, befitting the well-heeled patrons who remained for the entire season.

The famous coconut palms, which gave South Florida its symbol of tropical splendor, were said to have been started from nuts washed ashore at Palm Beach in the 1870 wreck of the Spanish brig *La Providencia*.

FERRY DOCKS & ROYAL POINCIANA HOTEL, PALM BEACH, FLA.

1650

Ferry boats, seen to the left and right in this view, departed from this dock on Lake Worth opposite the Royal Poinciana.

This ferry, which claimed to be the oldest ride on the Intracoastal Waterway, is passing the Hotel Alba, a competitor of the Flagler resorts. The structure has been rebuilt and now offers condominium residences.

Guests at Flagler's hotels were provided the most up-to-date facilities offering the popular recreational and social pursuits of the day. Here women participate in a tennis match on the hotel's courts c. 1900. (Courtesy of Florida State Archives.)

The Royal Poinciana's professionally designed golf course opened in 1897 and claimed to be Florida's first nine-hole course. It was later enlarged to 18 holes and is Florida's oldest 18-hole golf course today. Henry Plant's Belleview Hotel also touted its famed golfing facilities.

PALM BEACH, FLA    Grand Stand — Royal Poinciana.

Here a crowd gathers at the grandstand to watch a sack race competition. A second Breakers hotel (1904–1925) can be seen in the background.

53

PALM BEACH, FLA. Ball Room — Royal Poinciana.

The hotel's elegant ballroom offered formal evening entertainment, often to the accompaniment of the in-house orchestra. The highlight of the social year was Washington's Birthday Ball, held on February 22, at the height of the season. (Courtesy of Florida State Archives.)

The Everglades Club, Palm Beach, Florida

The Everglades Club on Lake Worth was an early creation of architects Addison Mizner and Paris Singer, who were in the forefront of South Florida's Mediterranean architectural transformation. Built in 1918, the club would gain a reputation as the top resort club in the United States.

Guests at Flagler's hotels, who often included prominent figures of the day, were provided with the most modern means of communication with the outside world during their stay in the remote Florida wilderness. This photograph shows telegraphers at a Florida East Coast Railway office in 1908. (Courtesy of Florida State Archives.)

This aerial view shows Flagler's Hotel Royal Poinciana in the foreground, his Whitehall residence to the right, and the second Breakers hotel in the background. The Royal Poinciana began to decline in the 1920s and was torn down in 1934. The lumber from the hotel was reportedly used to build private homes along the coast. (Courtesy of Florida State Archives.)

The Palm Walk that ran between the Royal Poinciana and The Breakers was reserved exclusively for pedestrians. Wheeled vehicles used the adjacent trail. Lined with palm trees and other exotic plantings, the walkway offered a shaded, scenic promenade for guests out for a stroll or a visit to the resort's seaside attractions.

Ask Mr. Foster? was the travel agent for Gilded Age tourists, with offices in major cities and resort locales. This Ask Mr. Foster? office was located across from the Royal Poinciana. Other locations included Flagler's Cordova Hotel in St. Augustine and Henry Plant's Tampa Bay Hotel. Services included travel arrangements by train or steam and hotel reservations and information, including "letters of introduction that will help to smooth your way."

Flagler built his second Palm Beach hotel, the Palm Beach Inn, directly on the shores of the Atlantic Ocean. As with the Royal Poinciana, guests arriving by rail were brought right to the hotel's door. The structure was planned to accommodate overflow guests from the Royal Poinciana, but it quickly gained popularity due to its beachfront location and informal style. In 1900, the hotel was enlarged and upgraded to a more luxurious status. It was renamed The Breakers, a term more descriptive of its location "down by the breakers." (Courtesy of Florida State Archives.)

The Breakers burned to the ground in June 1903 during an enlargement. Fortunately the fire occurred after the season, when few guests were in residence. (Courtesy of Florida State Archives.)

Flagler rehired his favored design firm, McGuire and McDonald, to give the new Breakers a grander appearance than its rustic predecessor. The mule car pictured here at the south entrance of the new hotel provided transportation around the grounds and between the hotels. The only alternative form of transportation on the island was bicycles and bicycle chairs, as Flagler would not allow horses or cars. (Courtesy of Florida State Archives.)

The second Breakers is pictured here from the west side, which overlooked the extensive grounds and the Hotel Royal Poinciana. Like its predecessor, the 1904 Breakers was a wooden structure. Not until fire destroyed the hotel for the third time in 1925 did the hotel's architects decide on a fireproof concrete construction. (Courtesy of Florida State Archives.)

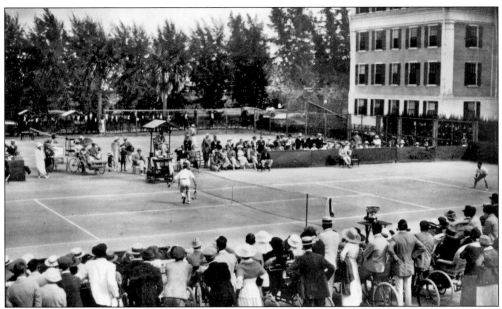

The grand hotels offered the most up-to-date facilities for engaging in the top competitive sports of the day—golf, tennis, and bicycling. Tournament play in progress here is being watched by guests seated in the resort's signature bicycle chairs, c. 1918. (Courtesy of Florida State Archives.)

The second, more luxurious Breakers gained a wide acceptance from Gilded Era tourists, as evidenced by this packed veranda during the 1905 season. (Courtesy of Florida State Archives.)

The Breakers dining room was festively decorated with tropical flora, while stylized parrots and birdcages hung from the ceiling.

The Port of Palm Beach, a 1,000-foot pier constructed in front of the Palm Beach Inn in 1896, allowed tourists to connect with Flagler steamboats leaving for Key West, Havana, and Nassau. Flagler owned two hotels in Nassau—the Colonial and Victoria—and later opened the Casa Marina in Key West. (Courtesy of Florida State Archives.)

The pier was a popular place for socializing or fishing and was often crowded with guests from both the Royal Poinciana and The Breakers. (Courtesy of Florida State Archives.)

Victorian attire is on full display in this photograph taken at Palm Beach c. 1910. (Courtesy of Florida State Archives.)

This panoramic view shows bathers enjoying the resort's major attraction—the wide sandy beachfront. Strict rules were enforced regarding bathing attire. Women were required to wear

Beach at the Casino, The Breakers Hotel,
Palm Beach, Florida.

Warm weather and blue skies drew midwinter crowds to the beach and the Casino, located next to The Breakers. A promotional brochure from the 1920s says "The Casino, containing one thousand dressing rooms, is a veritable temple of amusement from which the surf bathers descend through the concealed passageway to the beach." The hotel's orchestra provided musical accompaniment for the beachgoers.

black stockings with no flesh showing, and men had to cover their chests.

The resort's famed Roman pool was located adjacent to the Casino. (Courtesy of Florida State Archives.)

An interesting beach safety feature of the day was the use of life lines. (Courtesy of Florida State Archives.)

The life lines can be seen here to the left. Surf bathers could hold onto the line to avoid being swept to sea. Standard swimwear at the time of this 1918 photograph included bathing caps for women. (Courtesy of Florida State Archives.)

This aerial view of Flagler's Palm Beach resorts pre-1925 shows the beach, pool, and Casino buildings in the foreground, the second Breakers to the right, and the Royal Poinciana in the background. The line of foliage in the center is the Palm Walk, reserved for pedestrians, and the Pine Trail for the wheeled chairs and bicyclists. The two paths ran side by side between the hotels. This was originally the route of the train that came to the door of the two hotels. (Courtesy of Florida State Archives.)

On March 18, 1925, the day following St. Patrick's Day, The Breakers suffered its most disastrous fire. The hotel was totally destroyed at four in the afternoon during the height of the winter season. The blaze was discovered by a passerby who noticed heavy smoke pouring from the building. Within minutes, many of the approximately 1,000 guests were scrambling from the structure. (Courtesy of Florida State Archives.)

Shortly after the 1925 fire, the hotel's owners, heirs of Flagler's third wife, Mary Lily Kenan, decided to rebuild the structure in the manner of a grand Italian palace. The stated objective was to create the finest resort in the world. This view shows the third Breakers, completed in 1926 at a cost of over $6 million. The smokestack (left) from the power generation plant is the only structure on the grounds that survived all three fires. (Courtesy of Florida State Archives.)

The Kenan family selected renowned New York architect Leonard Schultze, designer of the Waldorf Astoria, to create the new Breakers. More than 1,200 craftsmen and 75 Italian artisans were hired to build the structure, which was finished in 11 months and 14 days. The hotel's Italian Renaissance architecture was inspired by the Villa Medici in Italy. This view of the lobby shows the magnificence of the hotel's design and appointments. (Courtesy of Florida State Archives.)

The Breakers's south porch, shown here shortly after the hotel's completion, looked across a green space to the Casino. The hotel's long tradition of classic elegance has been carried forth by the Kenan family in today's five-star resort. (Courtesy of Florida State Archives.)

The fountain that graces the dramatic entryway to The Breakers is an "almost replica" of the one in the Biboli Gardens of Florence, Italy. Instead of cherubs around the base, The Breakers' version features alligators and pelicans. (Courtesy of Florida State Archives.)

THE MAGIC OF THE GULF STREAM

PONCE DE LEON
ST. AUGUSTINE
ALCAZAR

ORMOND
HOTEL ORMOND

So long as the Gulf Stream flows up the *East Coast of Florida* — so long as the sun shines — the *East* Coast of Florida will be the most natural place to spend the winter. Thank Nature for the summer magic of that tropical current. Thank man for the vision to *see* and the courage to *make* of that *East* Coast of Florida a land of supreme attraction, a land for rest or play, for a nation of people to the North in the winter time.

ROYAL POINCIANA
PALM·BEACH
THE NEW BREAKERS

MIAMI

ROYAL PALM HOTEL

LONG KEY FISHING CAMP
LONG KEY

KEY WEST
CASA MARINA

EAST COAST OF FLORIDA

The Magic of the Gulf Stream is Winter's call to Play or to Rest on the *East* Coast of Florida. For rest and play the great resorts of the *East* Coast were made. Art and a tropical setting color the days. Fashion dresses them. And people, eager, alert, companionable, give them spirit. Select your own part. Every material facility is present for sport, in the water or on the land. And from Nature, herself, Rest—the *fountain of youth* or the *fountain of health*— under the magic spell of the Gulf Stream.

Of the many delightful Winter Resort Hotels on the *East Coast* of Florida, the rendezvous of Society at play have long been:—
*At* ST. AUGUSTINE
*Alcazar — Ponce de Leon*
*At* ORMOND
*Ormond-on-the-Halifax*
*At* PALM BEACH
*Royal Poinciana — Breakers*
*At* MIAMI
*The Royal Palm*
*At* LONG KEY
*Long Key Fishing Camp*
*At* KEY WEST
*Casa Marina*
Openings — Dec. 18th to Jan. 15th
All owned and operated on the American Plan by the
FLORIDA EAST COAST HOTEL COMPANY

Only 26 to 36 hours from North Eastern or Central States. The Florida East Coast Railway, now completely double-tracked to Miami, gives the *East* Coast resorts the only continuous double-track system from Eastern cities. Newest and best equipment, automatic block signals, etc., insure absolute safety and schedule time. All locomotives oil burning. Numerous de luxe trains, daily, scheduled for the winter months.
*For illustrated booklets of hotels, time tablet, etc., address*
Florida East Coast Railway Co.
Florida East Coast Hotel Co.
*(Flagler System)*
2 West 45th Street, NEW YORK or General Offices, St. Augustine, FLORIDA

Extensive advertising promoting the Flagler System hotels was placed in publications that reached the high-society audience targeted as clientele. This ad, which ran in *Harper's Bazaar* during the 1920s, featured the grand hotels in St. Augustine, Palm Beach, and Miami, as well as the Hotel Ormond, which Flagler bought in 1891, and the Casa Marina and Long Key Fishing Camp in the Florida Keys. (Courtesy of Seth Bramson, Miami Memorabilia.)

# *Three*

# MIAMI
## *Royal Palm Hotel*

Flagler chose an imposing site where the Miami River flows into Biscayne Bay as the location for his grand Royal Palm. The hotel became the center of Miami social activity as the newest destination for the rich and famous shortly after opening January 16, 1897.

PANORAMIC VIEW FROM ROYAL PALM HOTEL.

Miami was a struggling frontier village in 1895 when Flagler chose the town as the terminating point of his railroad. Building of the palatial Royal Palm Hotel brought instant prosperity and notoriety to Miami, and by the 1920s, the town had rapidly become the nation's tropical playground. This 1904 photograph shows the town of Miami as viewed from the hotel. (Courtesy of Florida State Archives.)

Groundbreaking for the Royal Palm took place on March 15, 1896, at its site at the mouth of the Miami River. As with the other Flagler hotels, the Royal Palm was constructed on a grand scale and became Miami's dominant feature. During the construction period in 1896, it is estimated that half of the town's 2,000 inhabitants worked for Flagler in some capacity. (Courtesy of Florida State Archives.)

The grand Royal Palm was an impressive sight surrounded by lushly landscaped tropical grounds and waterfront vistas. Architects James McGuire and Joseph McDonald, who Flagler had used to build his St. Augustine and Palm Beach hotels, moved south to supervise the Royal Palm's construction. The hotel featured the Colonial Revival style employed in the Royal Poinciana and the first two Breakers.

The Royal Palm's extensive grounds, shown here during the early stages of development, featured rare and native tropical plants, including plenty of the hotel's signature royal palms. The plantings were done by Henry Coppinger Sr., the city's first horticulturist and landscaper. (Courtesy of Florida State Archives.)

Miami social life centered around the hotel. Here a crowd gathers at Royal Palm Park for a flag ceremony in April 1922. The outline of the baseball diamond can also be seen. (Courtesy of Florida State Archives.)

DAILY BAND CONCERTS, MISS TRAVERSE, SOPRANO, MIAMI, FLA.

Afternoon band concerts, held daily during the season in the park, were a popular attraction for hotel guests and Miami residents.

Miami, Florida. Glimpse of Biscayne Bay, looking North.

The hotel grounds extended along the Miami River to Biscayne Bay, offering guests the opportunity to view the variety of commercial and recreational vessels around the busy harbor.

WM. JENNINGS BRYAN TALKING TO HIS SABBATH SCHOOL CLASS AT ROYAL PALM PARK, MIAMI, FLA.

As many as 5,000 people attended the world's largest Sunday school class, held weekly at Royal Palm Park. The sessions were led by William Jennings Bryan, the famous orator, preacher, and three-time Democratic presidential candidate. Flagler, a deeply religious man, provided worship opportunities for guests at each of his grand hotels.

The Royal Palm can be seen to the left in this early photograph showing the mouth of the Miami River. The river was a working waterway playing host to boat yards, fish houses, mills, and other commercial enterprises.

This later view shows the Royal Palm's dominant position in the Miami cityscape. The hotel remained the city's most prominent feature until the boom era of the 1920s.

Steamships owned by Flagler's Florida East Coast Railway connected passengers with the ports of Havana, Nassau, Key West, Palm Beach, and more northern locales. The extensive transportation and accommodations network built by Flagler allowed travelers to go first class throughout their journey. This 1899 photograph shows the steamer *City of Key West* heading out from the Royal Palm for a visit to the Keys. (Courtesy of Florida State Archives.)

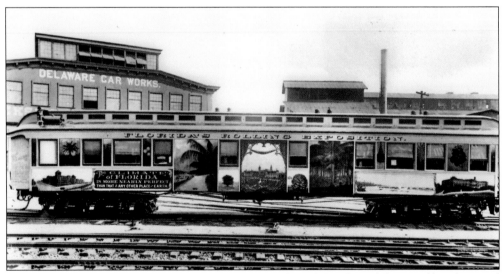

Flagler used this rolling exposition car to tout the wonders of Florida and the grand hotels up and down his Florida East Coast rail line. The scenes pictured on the car include tropical views as well as the Ponce de Leon and Royal Palm hotels. The car is parked in the yard of the Delaware Car Works in Wilmington, where Flagler's rail cars were manufactured. (Courtesy of Delaware Public Archives.)

Passengers on the Florida East Coast Railway's New York-to-Miami run are pictured here relaxing in the parlor car. (Courtesy of Florida State Archives.)

Baggage carts are loaded as tourists arrive at the Florida East Coast Railway Miami Depot in 1921. The city was the rail line's southern terminus for more than a decade, until the Key West extension opened in 1912, a year before Flagler's death. The Key West route was destroyed by a hurricane that struck on Labor Day 1935. (Courtesy of Florida State Archives.)

APPROACHING THE ROYAL PALM HOTEL THROUGH THE AUSTRALIAN PINES, MIAMI, FLA.

The automobile age had arrived in Florida as shown by this early-20th-century view of Model T hardtops and convertibles parked bumper-to-bumper on the approach to the Royal Palm. The Australian pines lining the roadway are an exotic species introduced in the early 19th century. They flourished for years until many were destroyed by freezes or eradicated due to environmental concerns.

Royal Palm Grounds,
Miami, Fla.

Landscaping included a wide variety of flowering plants as well as the royal palms from which the hotel took its name.

Copyright 1905 by the Rotograph Co.

A 15252  Interior, Hotel Royal Palm, Miami, Fla.

*Florence-*

The impressive, columned rotunda was the focal point of the hotel's interior public space. An aura of casual tropical splendor was created with potted palms surrounding the wicker furnishings. The hotel's dining areas, reading room, parlors, and services led off from the rotunda. (Courtesy of Florida State Archives.)

The Royal Palm's distinction of being at the country's southernmost population point brought some interesting events to its doorstep. This 1908 photograph marks the end of the first road trip traversing the state from Jacksonville to Miami. (Courtesy of Florida State Archives.)

Flagler's grand hotels operated as complete self-contained resorts, offering excursions and facilities that allowed guests to engage in a variety of activities. Here a group heads to a picnic at nearby Arch Creek Natural Bridge, apparently getting a sendoff from the brass band. (Courtesy of Florida State Archives.)

ELSER PIER FROM ROYAL PALM GROUNDS, MIAMI, FLORIDA.

Excursion trips into the Everglades were available from the pier on the hotel grounds.

Airboats, such as this vessel passing by the Royal Palm, were equally at home on the open river or traversing the vast Everglades that bordered Miami. (Courtesy of Florida State Archives.)

Gag postcards featuring tourists posing with props and painted backdrops were a favorite souvenir to send the folks back home.

These ladies are engaging in a game of clock golf; the sand "green" represented a clock face. The objective apparently was to putt toward the "time" markers on the perimeter. (Courtesy of Florida State Archives.)

Cumbersome Victorian attire worn by ladies of the day did not inhibit participation in sports that required agility such as golf. This activity on the Hotel Royal Palm front lawn c. 1899 appears to be drawing a number of spectators. (Courtesy of Florida State Archives.)

This bicycling group was referred to as the "Dirty Dozen," and included members of the Burdine family who founded Florida's landmark department store chain in Miami. Roddy Burdine is on the right, and Freeman Burdine is fifth from left. (Courtesy of Florida State Archives.)

A major attraction at the Royal Palm was the swimming pool managed by world-champion swimmer Percy F. Cavill. Aquatic exhibitions directed by Cavill were given regularly. Feats included greased-pole walking, racing, obstacle swimming, tilting in canoes, diving from springboards, somersaulting dives, fancy swimming in street clothes and in women's clothes, and swimming with the feet tied. (Courtesy of Florida State Archives.)

Guests seeking a relaxed form of amusement are pictured here utilizing the rockers that lined the hotel veranda. (Courtesy of Florida State Archives.)

Walkways through the Royal Palm's landscaped environs provided opportunities for a pleasant stroll. The message on this postcard, dated February 16, 1913, says "Wreck on the road held up trains 26 hours."

A short distance away from the hotel was the Seminole Club, opened by Julia Tuttle's son Henry in her former home after her death. The club featured gambling and also sold liquor, which violated his mother's wishes that no alcoholic beverages be allowed within the city limits. Henry also platted the remainder of the estate as a subdivision, which included Fort Dallas Park, going against Julia Tuttle's agreement with Flagler not to subdivide the property. (Courtesy of Florida State Archives.)

This photograph, taken January 22, 1929, shows a crowded parking lot at the Royal Palm a year before the hotel was condemned as termite ridden and unsound. The structure had been badly damaged in the hurricane of 1926 and lay vacant for several years before it was razed during the 1930s. (Courtesy of Florida State Archives.)

# *Four*

# TAMPA
## *Tampa Bay Hotel*

Henry Plant opened his grandest hotel, the Tampa Bay Hotel, in 1891 at Tampa, the terminus of his Plant System railroad. Styled as a Moorish castle with 13 domes and minarets, the hotel cost nearly $3 million to build and furnish. A stroll around the mammoth structure covered nearly a mile. Plant reportedly sent Henry Flagler an invitation to the hotel's grand opening, to which his East Coast rival sniffed, "Where's Tampa?" Plant responded, "Just follow the crowds!" (Courtesy of Florida State Archives.)

The Tampa Bay Hotel is pictured here under construction. The hotel took three years to build and opened to a grand celebration held February 5, 1891, to which over 2,000 guests were invited. The festivities, which lasted well into the night, featured a grand ball, fireworks display, and electric illumination of the building and grounds. An article in the next day's *New York Times* proclaimed the facility "one of the grandest in the country." (Courtesy of University of South Florida Library.)

This early view looking from the Tampa Bay Hotel toward the Hillsborough River shows only a few isolated structures, including the First Baptist Church under construction beside the hotel. Across the river now is downtown Tampa. (Courtesy of Florida State Archives.)

TAMPA BAY HOTEL,
TAMPA, FLORIDA, U.S.A.
A.E. DICK, MANAGER.

Plant chose John A. Wood, a respected but little-known New York architect, to design and build his crown-jewel property. Conceived on a grand scale, Plant expanded the structure twice during construction. When complete, the hotel contained over 500 rooms set on six acres of grounds. Today the hotel's grand legacy is preserved at the Henry B. Plant Museum, which shares the building with the University of Tampa. (Courtesy of Tampa–Hillsborough County Public Library System.)

Henry Plant made Tampa the terminating point of his railroad in 1884 and constructed Port Tampa, a deepwater port. He built the modest Inn at Port Tampa, shown here, to serve guests connecting on his rail and steamship lines. Plant's integrated network of railroad, steamship lines, and accommodations would fully flower with the opening of the Tampa Bay Hotel, his first grand-scale luxury property.

This portrait of Henry B. Plant, taken during his later years, is one of the few existing photographs of the famed empire builder. Plant shied from publicity and was rarely captured on film by photographers of the day. (Courtesy of the Henry B. Plant Museum.)

The Tampa Bay Hotel, Plant's flagship property, was featured in this ad for the Plant System hotels and rail line. The entire hotel was lighted by electricity, considered a rare luxury in that day. An elaborate boathouse, casino, and theatrical auditorium graced the grounds. The exotic, grand Tampa Bay Hotel has in recent years been referred to as Florida's first "Magic Kingdom." (Courtesy of Florida State Archives.)

Plant's second wife, Margaret, is shown here on the steps of the Tampa Bay Hotel. They were married in 1873, 11 years after the death of his first wife, Ellen Blackstone Plant. Margaret was one year younger than his son Morton. (Courtesy of the Henry B. Plant Museum.)

Here Tampa Bay Hotel's formally attired guests relax in the hotel rotunda, termed "the heart of the house" in a promotional brochure. Today the area serves as the foyer of the University of Tampa, which acquired the property for its campus in 1931. (Courtesy of Florida State Archives.)

No expense was spared in furnishing the rooms and parlors of Plant's showpiece hotel. Plant and his wife, Margaret, acquired nearly $1 million worth of period pieces for the hotel during a European tour. The interior of the lavish hotel was described by one writer as a "jewel casket into which has been gathered an infinite number of rare and exquisite gems of furniture from many lands." This view shows a parlor suite. (Courtesy of Florida State Archives.)

In the grand style, trains from Plant's railroad system brought guests to the hotel's rear entrance. Patrons with means would arrive by private rail car for an entire season's stay, accompanied by family members, servants, and belongings. This photograph shows a 1902 train departure. (Courtesy of Tampa–Hillsborough County Public Library System.)

A 15392 Veranda, Tampa Bay Hotel, Tampa, Fla

The spacious verandas overlooking the hotel's lush, expansive grounds were a popular gathering place for guests seeking the benefits of the warm Florida sunshine and salubrious air.

Concerts given each morning by the hotel orchestra on the west piazza were a popular attraction. (Courtesy of the Henry B. Plant Museum.)

These rickshaws, patterned after the Oriental conveyances, offered guests an exotic form of transportation around the hotel grounds. Hotel bellmen provided the locomotion. The vehicles appear to have been less popular than the wheeled chairs at Flagler's Palm Beach resorts.

The Tampa Bay Hotel's bellhops, shown here in a somewhat somber pose, worked summers at hotels in Atlantic City, New Jersey, where wheeled chairs were also popular. (Courtesy of the Henry B. Plant Museum.)

This view shows the Palmetto Walk through Plant Park and the docks along the Hillsborough River. The six acres of hotel grounds were populated with native palms and orange groves and also featured rare and exotic species that Plant imported from the Far East and tropical regions of the globe. Down the walk were the greenhouses where plants were nurtured and propagated. (Courtesy of Tampa–Hillsborough County Public Library System.)

These girls are seen peering out from one of the exotic species along the Palm Walk.

The Tampa Bay Hotel was a self-contained resort in the grand manner, providing top-line entertainment and recreational diversions for its guests, many of whom stayed for the entire season. This group of golfers is seen posing in front of the racetrack and exposition hall. (Courtesy of the Henry B. Plant Museum.)

This ad touts the hotel's many amenities, which offered excitements or rest and relaxation. Note the opportunity touted to drive over "150 miles of oiled shell roads."

This photograph provides a rare glimpse of Henry Plant (third from left, wearing sombrero) with a group preparing to play golf. The hotel's limited nine-hole course was a lesser attraction among the many sports pursued by guests. (Courtesy of the Henry B. Plant Museum.)

The hotel kennels, located on the grounds, provided dogs for hunting forays. "Gunners have every means to engage in their favorite sport," advised a promotional booklet. The brochure mentioned 10 varieties of game birds available, including snipe, quail, and plover. The game record for most birds killed in a day's shooting was listed at 117. (Courtesy of University of South Florida Library.)

The hotel boathouse, seen here on the right, offered sail and rowboats, described as being "in the charge of experienced and careful men." (Courtesy of Tampa–Hillsborough County Public Library System.)

The steamer *H. B. Plant* was a common sight on the Hillsborough River. The boat was owned by the Plant Investment Line until 1902 and offered passenger runs to nearby St. Petersburg as well as the Manatee River and Punta Gorda. It was later purchased by the Favorite Line. The vessel burned at a Tampa pier in 1913. (Courtesy of Florida State Archives.)

Top-name entertainers and groups appeared regularly at the Tampa Bay Hotel, billed as "larger than almost any New York theater," and "the first theatrical auditorium and stage in the South." (Courtesy of University of South Florida Library.)

This group is shown departing the casino following an afternoon program. The facility was outfitted with "handsome opera chairs" and seated 2,000 people. When not in use for theatrical productions, the casino floor was rolled back to reveal a 50-foot-by-70-foot swimming pool. The pool was attended by a swimming instructor as well as a ladies' maid and featured large dressing rooms, each with an outside view. (Courtesy of Tampa–Hillsborough County Public Library System.)

Tampa's first Gasparilla Coronation Ball was held at the hotel's ballroom in May 1904. (Courtesy of Tampa–Hillsborough County Public Library System.)

A signboard on the post at the entrance to the Tampa Bay Hotel advertises a comic act at the casino. The photograph was taken in 1898. (Courtesy of Florida State Archives.)

Entertainment was also offered at the nearby Tampa Opera House located downtown, just over the Hillsborough River from the hotel. (Courtesy of Tampa–Hillsborough County Public Library System.)

These entertainers are members of the Jenkins Orphanage Band from Charleston, South Carolina. The band traveled to raise funds for the orphanage, which was the first in South Carolina for black children. The band proved to be a fertile training ground for young musicians, a number of whom would go on to join noted jazz bands. The trombonist fifth from the right is said to be "Cat" Anderson of Duke Ellington Orchestra fame. (Courtesy of Florida State Archives.)

When the Spanish-American War broke out in 1898, Henry Plant used his considerable political clout to have the Tampa Bay Hotel named center of American operations for the conflict. The destination gained the hotel national prominence and assured Plant a full house during the war period. A group of officers is pictured here on the hotel porch. (Courtesy of Florida State Archives.)

Officers' wives stayed at the hotel with their families while their spouses participated in the war. This photograph of a group of wives and daughters was taken at the hotel's front entrance.

The famed de Soto Oak is said to be the site where the famous Spanish explorer Hernando de Soto camped when he came ashore on the west coast of Florida in 1539. The legend, according to some sources, maintains that de Soto made his treaty with the local natives under this very tree. (Courtesy of Tampa–Hillsborough County Public Library System.)

Following Henry Plant's death in 1899, his heirs showed little interest in operating the Tampa Bay Hotel and sold the property to the City of Tampa in 1905. The selling price was $125,000, a fraction of the hotel's $2-million construction cost. Pictured here is a grand promenade walk that ran the length of the hotel.

Under city ownership, the hotel grounds were renamed Plant Park and served as the site for civic events and gatherings as well as hotel-related functions. The grand hotel continued to prosper under city ownership until the Depression years. Here a group of ladies gather in the Tea Garden in the spring of 1923. (Courtesy of Tampa–Hillsborough County Public Library System.)

Plant's rail line, which became the Atlantic Coast Line railroad, provided first-class passenger service to Tampa and the hotel from Northern cities. Here, the "Tampa Special" is shown arriving at Union Station in 1922. (Courtesy of Tampa–Hillsborough County Public Library System.)

This group of Kiwanians is celebrating in the hotel's dining room *c.* 1927. (Courtesy of Tampa–Hillsborough County Public Library System.)

Tampa's annual Gasparilla celebration drew crowds every February at the height of the tourist season. The Tampa Bay Hotel benefited greatly from its proximity to the festival's events. (Courtesy of Tampa–Hillsborough County Public Library System.)

The grounds of Plant Park offered a perfect vantage point to view the arrival of the Gasparilla pirate ship. Here spectators can be seen gathered on the river's edge—at the Tampa Bay Hotel across the river and on the Atlantic Coast Line rail cars in the foreground—for the event in 1924. (Courtesy of Tampa–Hillsborough County Public Library System.)

Retirees who flocked to Florida and the Tampa area during the tourist- and land-boom days of the 1920s enjoyed sedate activities such as shuffleboard and lawn games. Here a group of tourists watch a shuffleboard tournament being played at the Tampa Tourist Center near the Tampa Bay Hotel. (Courtesy of Tampa–Hillsborough County Public Library System.)

Plant Park, in front of the hotel, was the site of numerous activities during the era of the city's ownership of the Tampa Bay Hotel and grounds. This 1922 photograph shows a horseshoe-pitching tournament in progress. A baseball game can be seen in the background. (Courtesy of Tampa–Hillsborough County Public Library System.)

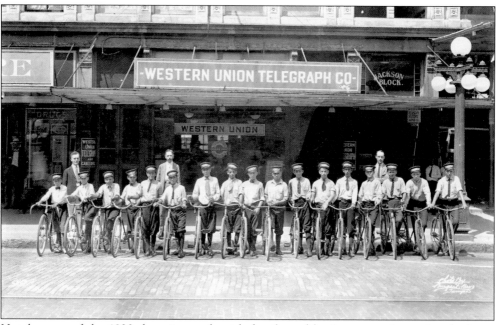

Hotel guests of the 1920s kept in touch with family and business associates via telephone and telegraph, the e-mail of the day. Western Union messengers were ready to offer speedy delivery of telegrams from the company's downtown Tampa location. (Courtesy of Florida State Archives.)

The Tampa Theater, located downtown across the river from the hotel, offered the latest in motion picture entertainment. The theater is shown here in 1929 trumpeting the current innovation—movies with sound. (Courtesy of Tampa–Hillsborough County Public Library System.)

Madam Himes brought her beauty parlor to the Tampa Theater lobby to promote a hairdo tie-in with popular film star Clara Bow. The sign reads, "Enjoy the new Clara Bow haircut, then be our guest to enjoy Clara Bow in *Love Among the Millionaires*." (Courtesy of Tampa–Hillsborough County Public Library System.)

Sulphur Springs was a popular recreation venue for tourists and Tampa residents alike. The daunting high dive on the left apparently had no takers when this photograph was taken on a crowded afternoon in 1922. (Courtesy of Tampa–Hillsborough County Public Library System.)

The alligator was the icon of early Florida tourism, and the gator pens at Sulphur Springs were a featured attraction. Note the warning: "Annoying Alligator Not Allowed." (Courtesy of Tampa–Hillsborough County Public Library System.)

# *Five*

# BELLEAIR
## *Hotel Belleview*

Henry Plant built his second grand hotel, the Swiss chalet-style Belleview, in 1896 on a high bluff overlooking Clearwater Bay. Plant envisioned the hotel as the focal point of a planned community that he called Belleair. He brought a spur of his railroad right to the hotel's entrance, assuring convenient access for the wealthy tourists and sportsmen who were his targeted clientele. The Belleview, which would come to be known as "The White Queen of the Gulf," was painted brown in the beginning. The hotel acquired its characteristic white color when repainted by Plant's son Morton after he inherited the property in 1900. This photograph shows the hotel in its early days shortly after construction. (Courtesy of Heritage Village Archives and Library.)

Newly planted palms line the entryway leading up to the Belleview in this photograph taken shortly after the hotel's completion. Though located in the Florida wilderness, the Belleview featured the most up-to-date amenities, including electricity generated by the steam plant on the left. An early promotional brochure promised three electric lights in every guest room. (Courtesy of Heritage Village Archives and Library.)

The Belleview Grounds, Looking South

The area surrounding the Belleview was remote and undeveloped, offering the opportunity for the creation of landscaped grounds with paths and roadways leading off in all directions. The railroad spur can be seen in the foreground of this view looking south. (Courtesy of Heritage Village Archives and Library.)

BELLEAIR, FLA. *This is a delightful corner of the world to rest in —* A. B. B.

Tampa architects Michael J. Miller and Francis J. Kennard designed the Belleview in the Swiss chalet-style architecture popular in American and European resort areas. The style is characterized by pointed gables and overhanging roofs. The hotel offered 145 rooms, a large dining room, and public areas. A bakeshop and billiard room were downstairs. This card's inscription reads, "This is a delightful corner of the world to rest in." (Courtesy of Heritage Village Archives and Library.)

Belleair, Fla. Belleview Hotel Grounds, main entrance, driveway and cottages

A group of 12 cottages—actually mini-mansions—surrounded the Belleview and were available for rental by the wealthy socialites who would spend the entire winter season at the hotel with their entourage, which would often include family, friends, and servants. The cottages were built by individuals on hotel property with the understanding that the hotel would assume ownership of them after five years. Thereafter the former owners paid rent to use the cottages. (Courtesy of Heritage Village Archives and Library.)

# WEST COAST HOTELS
## OF FLORIDA.

Owned and Operated by the **Plant System.** Under Management of Mr. D. P. HATHAWAY.

# HOTEL BELLEVIEW,
### BELLEAIR, FLA.

Beautifully situated. Over-looking the Gulf of Mexico. Fine Fishing and Hunting, Boating and Sailing. . . .

OPENED JANUARY 15TH, 1897.

RATES UPON APPLICATION.

**W. A. BARRON, Resident Manager,**
. . . . BELLEAIR, FLA.

As part of the Plant System that included Henry Plant's railroad, steamship line, and hotels, the Belleview received extensive advertising support from the beginning. This ad touts the hotel in its inaugural 1897 season. (Courtesy of Heritage Village Archives and Library.)

The original bridge leading over Corkscrew Creek to the hotel was an ornate arched structure with shops on the lower level selling souvenirs and candy. A railroad bridge was located nearby. (Courtesy of Heritage Village Archives and Library.)

A new bridge with a gatehouse is pictured in this view from around 1920. Automobiles and carriages shared the entry bridge to the Belleview grounds at that time. The sign declares a speed limit of 18 miles per hour. (Courtesy of University of South Florida Library.)

Guests entered the hotel through the spacious lobby. This 1916 photograph shows a large check-in area and rather sparse furnishings. Located just off the lobby were telephone, telegraph, and newsstand facilities, where guests could keep in touch with the outside world. The hotel's house orchestra would often serenade guests in the lobby. (Courtesy of Heritage Village Archives and Library.)

The Belleview's public areas were decorated in a casual country fashion, contrasting the formal Victorian parlors seen at Plant's Tampa Bay Hotel. The west lounge, pictured here, featured wicker furnishings and a wall of windows that took full advantage of the Florida sunshine. (Courtesy of Heritage Village Archives and Library.)

The Belleview's grand Tiffany Dining Room was so-called because of the exquisite leaded-glass panels that graced the ceiling, created in the style of Louis Tiffany. The dining room was enlarged during a 1910 hotel renovation and currently serves as a ballroom and banquet facility. (Courtesy of Heritage Village Archives and Library.)

Guests were well looked after by a large hotel staff. This dormitory was built in 1897, concurrent with the hotel, to house workers at the Belleview who departed after the season for employment at Northern resorts. The building contained over 150 rooms and was comparable in size to one of the hotel's wings. A strict regimen of rules governed staff conduct and behavior. Dress codes and punctuality were strictly enforced, and violators were fined (25¢ was the norm). (Courtesy of Heritage Village Archives and Library.)

The first addition to the Belleview, shown here under construction before 1905, extended the main corridor eastward. Another major expansion occurred around 1910, when the north wing was built and the Tiffany Dining Room enlarged to its present size. In 1924, the addition of the south wing increased the hotel's capacity to 425 total rooms. (Courtesy George Fulmer.)

Guests could relax and socialize in the tea garden located on the south lawn. At this time, the hotel was known as the Belleview Biltmore, having been purchased by the Biltmore chain in 1919 after the death of Morton Plant.

Formal plantings, like the palms and cedars shown in this view from the north portico, lined the Belleview's walkways, giving the grounds a country-estate appearance. Plant used native vegetation in landscaping the resort's extensive grounds, as the sandy soil in the area would not support the exotic species that decorated the Tampa Bay Hotel's environs. (Courtesy of Heritage Village Archives and Library.)

The cedars have grown up to form the Cedar Walk leading to the north entrance in this 1920s photograph.

One of the Belleview's attractions was its location on Clearwater Bay, just a short boat ride from the Gulf of Mexico. This photograph was taken from the boathouse/bathing pavilion located on the pier. (Courtesy of Heritage Village Archives and Library.)

The structure at the end of the pier housed a freshwater spring that supplied the hotel's drinking water. The spring was considered a rarity because of its location in the midst of the saltwater bay. The man in the foreground appears to be perplexed, possibly because his sailboat has been landlocked due to the low water. (Courtesy of Heritage Village Archives and Library.)

Boats departing from this boathouse located on the pier took hotel guests on fishing and sightseeing trips and out to the hotel's beach property located on the nearby Sand Key barrier island. This view shows the boathouse/bathing pavilion c. 1900. (Courtesy of Heritage Village Archives and Library.)

The Belleview's isolated location in the Florida wilds offered plenty of opportunity for solitude, as this man's contemplative pose suggests. A fish net appears to be draped on the rocks. The hotel, pier, and springhouse can be seen in the background in this turn-of-the-century view. (Courtesy of Heritage Village Archives and Library.)

Fishing was a big deal for many hotel guests. Here a crowd gathers around the catch of the day—a large sawfish incorrectly identified as a "sword fish." (Courtesy of Heritage Village Archives and Library.)

The hotel's Olympic-sized swimming pool was inlaid with over one million ceramic tiles imported from Italy and held 200,000 gallons of water. In 1920, a year after its completion, the pool was used for Olympic swimming trials. (Courtesy of Heritage Village Archives and Library.)

The Belleview recreational amenities are featured in this 1906 advertisement. The hotel was being promoted as "the centre of winter golf" even before the 18-hole courses were completed in 1915. The early automobile loaded with occupants gives testimony to an era when driving was considered a sport.

Golf was an important hotel amenity from the beginning. Plant chose designer Launcelot Cressy Servos to create the hotel's original six-hole course in 1898, claimed to be Florida's first hotel golf course. In this *c.* 1898 photograph, a gentleman tees off on the original course. At that time, the greens were covered with crushed shell, and the shelters had thatched roofs. (Courtesy of Heritage Village Archives and Library.)

In 1915, well-regarded designer Donald J. Ross was picked by Morton Plant to create two 18-hole courses, giving the resort its reputation as a golfer's paradise. This 1920 photograph shows the fourth green on the west course. Access to the green was by the stairs on the left. (Courtesy of Heritage Village Archives and Library.)

Golfing greats of the day, such as Bobby Jones and Walter Hagen, frequented the courses, which were famed for their innovative design and challenging play. Here a crowd watches professional golfers wrap up tournament play on the 18th green c. 1916. Plant shipped in trainloads of topsoil from Indiana to enable the growth of grass on the sandy soil. (Courtesy of Heritage Village Archives and Library.)

The golf clubhouse was the place to gather a foursome or relax after a round of play. It was built in the bungalow style similar to that of the homes being constructed around the hotel at that time. (Courtesy of Heritage Village Archives and Library.)

Belleview advertising in the 1920s featured the golf course along with other hotel amenities like concerts, dancing, horse riding, water sports, and proximity to the Gulf of Mexico. This ad ran in *Country Life*, a publication catering to wealthy socialites of the day.

This postcard view of the Belleview shows the proximity of the "golf grounds" to the hotel, but no mention is made of errant balls smashing any windows. The hotel at this time included the east extension but not the north and south wings. (Courtesy of Heritage Village Archives and Library.)

Sandboxes were a favorite play place for children in the early 20th century. Many children spent the season with their parents at the Belleview and received special attention in the children's dining room and on-site school. The somber expressions on most of the kids' faces probably reflects their unhappiness with having to hold still for the photographer. (Courtesy of Heritage Village Archives and Library.)

These cyclists are members of the Eldredge Club, international bicycle champions from England. They are pictured here on the Belleview track *c.* 1900. The bicycle track was also used for horse racing during the 1898–1899 season. (Courtesy of Heritage Village Archives and Library.)

This group, probably hotel guests, is ready to set out on a bike ride. Formal attire was the norm for Victorian ladies and gentlemen, even in casual situations and warm climate. The photograph was taken *c.* 1900. (Courtesy of Heritage Village Archives and Library.)

Hotel guests out for a bicycle ride pause on the terraced lawn at the west end of the hotel. This spot offered a commanding view overlooking Clearwater Bay with the Gulf of Mexico in the distance. (Courtesy of Heritage Village Archives and Library.)

The Hotel Belleview, employee quarters (right), and millionaire cottages (back) can be seen in this aerial view. A train can also be spotted passing by the hotel. This somewhat fanciful drawing also shows what appears to be the golf clubhouse (by the flagpole), but no evidence of the golf course is seen. The card is postmarked January 24, 1916. At this time, the hotel's south wing had not yet been constructed.

An excursion to the Belleview's beachfront property at nearby Sand Key was a popular venue for guests. Boats left the hotel pier regularly for the trip across Clearwater Bay to the gulf. This 1926 photograph shows a group of picnickers listening to records while snacking on bananas. (Courtesy of Tampa–Hillsborough County Public Library System.)

Bathers soak up the surf and sun during a visit to the beach at Sand Key. The Belleview beach property is now the site of the Cabana Club condominiums. The adjacent restaurant and patio still supply beach access to hotel guests. (Courtesy of Tampa–Hillsborough County Public Library System.)

Coe Casino, situated conveniently just outside the Belleview grounds, offered high-stakes gambling to wealthy guests who were whisked by limousine to its door. An upscale dining room on the ground floor featured gourmet meals, while roulette wheels, slot machines, and other games of chance were in action upstairs. The casino did a flourishing business in the 1920s and 1930s but was closed during World War II and shuttered for good following a well-publicized raid in 1949. (Courtesy of Heritage Village Archives and Library.)

Military aircraft flew over the Belleview during World War II when the hotel was requisitioned as a training facility for armed forces personnel. (Courtesy of Heritage Village Archives and Library.)